Pressing Towards The Mark

It's not what you think

Written by:
Toresa M. Blakely

Copyright © 2011 Toresa M. Blakely
ISBN: 978-0-615-60031-4
Published by In Life Now Enterprises
636 Bates St. SE
Grand Rapids, MI 49503

Printed in the U.S.

Table of Contents

Dedication

To all of my dear children who have taught me so much in this life. I'd like to say thank you. I honor every one of you from the ones that came out of my womb to those that were a gift to me for a season. Terry Jr., Tiffanie, Sebastian, Majesty, Bryan Jr., Shari, Jacquard, and Charity remember I will always love you.

To my dearest Bryan, you always cause me to spread my wings and fly so that I soar like an eagle to the heights that are destined for me. Thank you for believing in me, pushing me, and for teaching me a lot about life with all the lessons it brings.

Introduction

Pressure is the driving force that pushes us into purpose. Pressing says I am not going to stay where I am. Pressure says that there is more for my life than what I currently see. Pressing says that I am going to get it. Pressure says pursue. Pressing says you must recover all.
There is a driving force in all of us. It says I am pressing towards the mark. This force says that I am going to make it. This force says even though you feel like giving up, you have got to keep going...

Many times in our lives, what we think we are pressing for turns out to be not what we are pressing for. Pressing after things that you feel are going to make you better is not it. Pressing after having a lot of money is not it. Pressing on your job so that you can be the top person in the company is not it. Pressing after things that give self-gratification is not it. Pressing after riches is not it. Pressing after that fine car and that fine house is not it. Sure having all these things are nice and who doesn't want to have them. We all do but guess what. Our mark in that press does not give us any true happiness. We find that it is only a temporary fix for what we are lacking spiritually, physically, and mentally.
People go through life achieving all these things but never finding true happiness. No matter what you do, it seems like you always have a feeling of emptiness and worthlessness after you have achieved all of these great accomplishments. I hear someone asking why is there a feeling of emptiness and worthlessness? Well I will tell you. The reason that people feel this way is because once they get or achieve those accomplishments that they were working so hard to achieve, they find out that it was not what they thought it was going to be. It did not make them

feel the way that they thought it was going to make them feel. Sure, you might be making more money on your job or you may have done pretty well with your new business venture, but you have discovered that your happiness was not found in these temporal things. You figured out that your worth is not in things.

So much of our life and so much of our energy and time is spent on things that really are not worth the effort that we are putting into them. We could have spent that precious time doing something that was much more profitable than continuing to put our confidence in the things of our flesh that are of this world. Too much precious energy was used on something that was not going to profit you anything in your spirit man. I hear some of you say, how can you say that Toresa? The answer is this. What does it profit you to gain the whole world but in the process of gaining the world, you lose your soul.

It boils down to this. It profited you nothing. You gained the world, you gained the business, you gained the riches, you gained the house, and you gained the world but you lost your soul. *You lost you in the process*.

You have pressed toward the mark and have found out that it is not what you thought it was going to be.

Chapter 1:   When you are just trying to be you

The writer Paul said in the book of Philippians in the third chapter verses twelve through fourteen, "forgetting those things that are behind me, I press towards the prize of the high call…"

Well everyone the time has come for me to tell another story that will bring conscientiousness you had not really pondered seriously. I believe in my heart you all will like this one. This book is not about me but has everything to do with and is connected to personal development and some dysfunctional types of learned behavior that we all are guilty of indulging in. In observations I have experienced while working with people and watching them from afar, I have discovered that we as people have had tendencies to press after things (you fill in the blanks) that was simply just a waste of our precious time and energy. However, most of the time we don't realize in that current situation or context how much of a waste it was until after we've attained. Once, we achieved it and looked at all of what we lost in order to get it, then we realized all of the emphasis we once put into getting it was not worth our efforts at all.

In the next few pages of this book, I will share some stories and/or thoughts with you that I hope cause you to really think about what your purpose in life really is. I want you to really begin to think about some of the things you are doing and how you are spending your time. This book is not intended for those individuals who have found themselves lost after achieving or getting something in their lives that they thought would fill some type of void. It is for every reader to take, read, and begin to examine the moral fabric and possible decay of our lives. I want you to take some time and set it aside to really look at some thoughts being presented to you and realign yourself. It is time to begin to change the way that you think. And let me just warn you right now, this book is not what you think it's going to be.

For many of us, I believe this is where the real struggle begins. I believe that it begins with us. When you are "just trying to be you" that can sometimes lead into a real battle to act and to be who we really are. I have made some observation over the years and have come to discover that most people are trying to act like someone they are not. The real issue is that we are struggling with an identity crisis. Why don't we feel comfortable in our own true identity? Why are we not comfortable in our own skin? Why do we keep walking around trying to please everyone? Why do we consistently keep acting like people we are not? I personally have come to the conclusion that it is ok just to be me, period! And if someone doesn't except me for being me then to hell with them! Why should I care about what others think about me if I am totally confident and comfortable with who I am. Let me be perfectly clear on this. You should be confident and comfortable in the person you were designed and created to be by the "Creator" himself while being formed in the womb not that idea of someone who people have carved you into being, which is someone who is fake, false, and contrived into being.

People in general have gotten themselves so caught up in being people pleasers instead of pleasing themselves and making sure that they are happy. However, it is in my opinion that the world has given us this persona that if you don't have a lot of people chasing after you or around you all the time then you are not a significant person that makes a difference. However, I beg to differ from that thought! How off in our thinking could we possibly be? This is another reason why not only are folks suffering from an identity crisis but it is also diagnosed as depression and rejection. Many men and women around the world feel like they are insignificant and that nobody really cares about them. Can I ask a question, a real question and you really think about it and answer it honestly for you? Why is it so important for many of you to be with the so called "in crowd" and make the outsider who is not a part of this community feel like they are not worth anything? Many of us have unknowingly become so pompous in our attitudes and how we carry ourselves to such a degree that it has become downright disgusting. I mean really, who do you think you are? Why do many of us feel like we can put ourselves up on a false unstable pedestal and then put on this impression that tries to exemplify that we are the kings and queens of all things above others?

This, I believe is why a lot of our young people have been crying out because they are not being accepted and embraced for the person they were created to be. Let me preface; when I say embraced for the person they are, I mean looking past whatever they may be doing which brings negativity but looking into the core of that young man or woman and discerning the beauty residing in them. Maybe if we learned how to do that and cultivate them in that area of their lives many of us would not experience so much of the pure drama they don't mind bringing our way at all. It is part of my opinion that our youth have picked up these prideful and/or exceedingly arrogant attitudes to the degree that they think they are kings and queens of something when in reality they are not because of us, the adults who are supposed to know who they are. Our youth are placing more value into having things rather than putting value into who they really are and how they could be affecting the lives of those that are around them like many of the adults they are pattering their lives around. How did they get this way? Well I believe one of the things that happened is because of us, the older people or those that are supposed to be the role models in the communities that we are living in.

To many times in our own neighborhoods and communities our youth see nothing that really stands out as being a positive influence where they see the adults simply accepting people for who they really are. Where is the love? Has anyone ever wondered about that? Where is the love? Why do we keep talking about people and have all of these great ideas on how to help but nobody ever puts anything into action or remains consistent in their efforts. Where is the love that is supposed to be shared with our brothers and our sisters regardless of what they look like, regardless of what their skin color is, regardless to whatever their addictions, regardless to their lifestyle preference? Ask yourself for real, where is the love? Begin to ask yourself, why do I keep walking around acting like I am a bag of chips and all that and yet I continue to treat those around me who are in no way like me like they are insignificant and mean nothing to the world?

When we as individuals or groups do this, we push people into a pit. We may not realize it but we do by our actions of being high minded, thinking that we are more than what we really are. Here is a thought that will begin to challenge you even more; if we could literally look into the lives of those people we perceive to be someone to esteem highly for just a day, we as individuals would soon find out that that person or those groups of people are no better than us. Why are they no better than us? It is because the majority of people in the world today are going through an identity crisis and instead of putting value into who we are as our own unique selves, we place the value of who we are with emphasis on things we have or things that we've accomplished. In addition, let the truth be told, most of us have not really done anything that has touched or really impacted the life or lives of those that are in our own families or communities we live in.

It is my desire at this particular point in life to bring awareness to you that you had not even thought about. When you are trying to be you these are some of the struggles people are going through or shall I say dealing with. It is hard for some people to be accepted for the person that the Creator created them to be. Why can't people just accept you at face value for who you are and what you choose to do in life?

One of the places in life where this struggle is very prevalent is in the so-called organized church of the 21st century. If the church is supposed to be a place of refuge, a place of healing, and a place of restoration, and a place of acceptance then why do we have so many people struggling in the house of God with who they are? They are struggling because they are trying to find or become themselves and be accepted, while not being able to fit in all the *clicks* that are running through our churches like wildfire destroying the very fiber of their true witness. I believe this is one of the very reasons why there is a revolving door when it comes to individuals stepping in the houses of faith across the country because when they come in, they immediately see through all of the trickery and phoniness being presented to them as "the love of Christ" so in turn they walk right back out! They see people falsely acting as if they are perfect and have it all together, while all the while they to are people struggling because they are not walking in their true identity either. They are not being their true selves but are continuously acting like someone they admire possibly; who they think has got it all together and sure of their self. Listen, those people too are struggling in their own personal identity crisis as well.

In my personal experience over the years, it has been my observation of seeing the so called church preaching the gospel of the kingdom, which is the good news of salvation, to preaching and teaching a falsehood of this prosperity message which says "stuff" makes you somebody! Can you believe this mess? Who would have ever thought of all places these lies would be told from the pulpits of churches across America and filter down into the pews of the churches in your community. They have brainwashed people into believing that if you are not tithing, driving nice cars, living in big houses, have oodles of money like the pastor that you and your precious life is of no significance. You are left to feel like you must be doing something wrong? How absurd? Now this area really bothers me because I personally was once on the receiving end of this type of dogma. I have been in churches where more emphasis was put on having things and manipulating me into giving money, while they (church leadership) portrayed themselves to me as if they were pictures of success while the "real" folks in the pews struggled with just trying to be themselves and be secure in it. I realize some of you may think I am being a bit harsh but I know for a fact that my viewpoint is representative of many who are still currently struggling. I only want to challenge you in your thinking to begin to really think about what we as people are subjecting ourselves to, which can sometimes influence how we try to figure out "just trying to be me."

I believe there is an invisible pressure placed on our church leadership, which has been projected over the years that forces their hands at becoming something they never ever were in the first place. This has evolved into a false learned behavior because even they themselves didn't come in the church being the fake people we see today. They just want to be who they are but are suffering with a severe case of identity delusion. They came in one way, saw how the sick church body was functioning and believed this was the acceptable behavior and then they picked up these learned ways that were not very *Christ-like* at all. All of this happening right in the church and we the people in these churches keep acting like everything is ok. It's not! When will people begin to wake up and begin to address this behavior? Do we even have to wonder anymore why people are suffering with depression and other mental ailments right in our spiritual hospitals, while not receiving mental loving cures, which can assist in stabilizing the sickness among us. But still we continue to elude the facts of the realities in which our people are dealing with or going through as they struggle to just be themselves. Why do we keep telling lies while in the midst we are guilty of stealing the people's vision?

Why do you have to struggle with just trying to be you? Why do you have to keep living a life that you know is a lie? Why do we keep playing mind and word games with people? Why can't we just be who we are and be shown the love, which we all need. Now, I am not badmouthing the church because we need the church but it is time for the church to come strong with some correction in the houses of God across America for we are losing people right under our noses and we need to understand some of the reasons why. Here is a thought I would like to present, if we are losing people in our spiritual hospitals who are already a part of the church community at astronomical numbers, can you imagine how ineffective we are with those who have not even stepped through the door of a church?

I believe it is past time to sound the alarm loud and clear right now and let people know that it is ok if you are driving a "hoopty." It is ok if you are riding the bus. It is ok if your house is not all that great or you live in an undesirable apartment or neighborhood. It is ok if you work a minimum wage job. It is ok if you made a mistake and had a child out of wedlock, the child is a blessing. It is ok if you are in the welfare system and receive food stamps or cash assistance. It is ok that you might not be living like someone you may know who lives in an affluent neighborhood. It is ok that you are not like everybody else but so much of your own self. Let me tell you again, it is ok! The point I desire to drive home right here is this, even though you may be dealing with one or all of these scenarios I just presented to you, you don't have to stay there in your thinking. Those things or places or people do not define who you are or who you have been created to be from your Creator! If you would only just believe in yourself regardless of your surroundings or circumstances may be. I want you to know that you do not have to struggle anymore with just being you. It's ok that you may be in these situations for now but I need you to keep in mind that these circumstances, places, people, and things have absolutely nothing to do with you as a person and who you are as your own unique beautiful individual! You do not have to change for anyone but yourself as you grow and development in your own personal development. I want you to do the hard internal work from within and evict all of the negative things you are dealing with internally because you feel people won't or will not accept you for "just being you." You no longer have to succumb to that bondage anymore! It's ok and guess what beloved, you are ok. I need you to know in your heart that things are going to get better and that you are perfectly fine with where you are right now because you are coming back to your true self. You are who you are and everything is ok! Your foundation for life is being laid right now as you read the words being shared to you through this book and you are being set free form this false bondage that has tried to captivate your life for far too long. This too shall pass but the biggest part of this revelation I want you to embrace is that you are now learning how to be comfortable in your own skin, simply being you and no one else but you.

This is the prize beloved. This was never supposed to be about your identity or worth and place of self-worth being defined by people, places, and things. The prize is when you discover who you are. This is the key unlocking the door to freedom in your mind. Your Creator doesn't put any more value into you if you have acquired a lot of riches or things. Value has been placed in you because you are uniquely you and there is nobody else on the face of this earth like you! For many of you, you need to start praising God right there because you finally can begin to see a little more clearly now. I want you to understand that it is ok to just be you. Learn how to accept you and love yourself for who God made you to be.

The struggle is not in the things, the struggle is not you, the struggle that you must overcome is learning how to put value into who you are and knowing in your heart that in spite of what others may say or do, you are somebody. You are somebody special. I love you and even more important than that, God loves you even more…
Your struggle is now over with just being you. Accept you, all of you, the good, the bad, and the ugly regardless of how people may treat you, accept you, or talk about you. Listen and hear me clearly beloved, you have just been delivered and set free. Your struggle is over. You are free to be you and only you, period!

Chapter 2:   When your mate doesn't understand

In your pursuit of happiness and pressing towards the mark there is something you personally need to accomplish and your mate does not understand. Yes, you love them and you desire nothing but the best in your relationship but there is something within you, which you are very passionate about doing. It is the force which drives you. You are literally living and breathing this force because it keeps you. It can sustain you if you could just immerse yourself completely into it. You must achieve and accomplish the tasks within you.

Your mate will support you because they love you but really, they don't understand. When this happens, a breach comes within the relationship because you failed to include them I what you sense, feel, and see causing them to oftentimes feel insignificant and irrelevant in the picture that you see. Your mate must feel included in what you are doing. You need to talk about your dreams, plans, and vision of what you desire to do while making sure they are completely included. Sometimes they will be able to give you a fresh perspective on what you are doing, which can aide you in doing it even better.

Let me share a little so that you can embrace what I am sharing with you. Way before I knew my husband, I knew my life would be used to do some great things which would help people as a whole and on an individual basis. There was a generational curse in my family line which had no other alternative but to stop its course of action with me because I commanded it to through my actions. I knew that my life had to be significant because I went through some very tough times and the enemy tried to literally kill me. I always knew that I had a story to tell, things to do, people to see, and places to go.

However, just because I knew that didn't mean that

after I got married my husband was going to see what I see, know it, believe it, let alone support it. When you get married, you must have candid conversations with your mate, which are genuine and innocent as you both share from your hearts but in your sharing can cause them to feel as if they are included in the grand scheme of things.

The two of you can be as different as night and day. and that is perfectly ok. This is what makes your union with your mate so unique. You have to begin to observe, listen, learn, and understand how the two of you operate and co-exist in your relationship together.

I have come to a place my relationship with my husband now where I understand how he flows and vice versa. My husband knows when it is time for me to get some rest and will encourage me to do so as I know when he is doing too much and will tell him he needs to slow down and prioritize his time. I must say however, it was not always like that, because when you go from being single to married you have got to learn how to get a balance on things. Life is different now and you must learn how to cohabitate with one another. We are talking about learning behaviors and communication styles with the most important person in our lives. I'll talk about being single later but let me just share with you now that when you are coming out of your singleness and entering into the union of holy matrimony some things you used to do in your singleness will have to change. Maybe I'll say it like this, you will have to learn how to re-adjust from single to full-time partner.

For example when I was single I could spend hours laying before the presence of the Lord. I would go through my daily routine but always took time to make sure I was centered in my faith through personal private time with my Creator. As I look back over my life, I must say I am truly thankful for that time because it was in those formative years of my spiritual walk with God where my foundation was being formed within the core of my very being.

Now, many of you who are reading this will obviously have a different interest than I but the point is "your thing you do" and how you can mesh it all together while remembering you are no longer by yourself anymore but have someone else in your life to think about and take into consideration. You must learn to compromise and re-adjust your life when you get married because your mate might not (and let me just be real) understand you for a moment after you first get married. You will have to learn how to listen to one another and talk things out. Communication is the key when your mate doesn't understand.

Now let me talk to you as a married woman now. I have learned how to put everything in its proper perspective. I now understand the importance of including my man first in all things because he causes me to operate in excellence due to the fact that he totally and completely believes in me and my vision for life. For me this is how it works and it works well. As it should be and I in turn am the same way with him, you should interact with your spouse. We talk about our needs, wants, and desires of life so that the other is included and can give insight or help bring clarity to our dreams. In turn we each feel totally committed to pushing the other into what they are supposed to be doing therefore causing both of us to feel totally included in each other's lives. I understand now that I can't be so engulfed in my things where I neglect my husband and not spend any time with him. He must feel like he is worth my time as well. He needs to know that yes, he has a woman who loves her God but also knows how to let husband know that she loves him too. Do you understand what I am saying? I think we tend to go overboard sometimes. We don't mean any harm but we can get so involved in what we are doing that we push our mates' to the side and push them right out of the picture. It has been my observation that this is one of the areas where we can unknowingly place a breach in our relationships with our mates. In your relationship with your mate you should not be so consumed to where you begin to neglect them in giving them the attention that they need from you as well. But this is what happens when your mate does not understand... Where is your friend? Where is your lover? Where is the one you used to adore? Where is the one who used to adore you? I implore you beloved to examine yourself and learn how to re-adjust your passions and pour some of that same energy back into your relationship with your mate.

In the process of pursuing the things which are within us to do, we also must ensure we are pursuing our mates by making sure we are not only giving them what they need but in turn they are also giving us what we need. Remember you need to prioritize the importance and make separate what is most important to your life and in your life. Please hear me clearly as I share this with you. There are things attached to your life which are important that you must carry out which is a part of your purpose and call from the divine, and then there are the important intricacies within your marriage you need in your life like your mate. You cannot expect to go out and lead others in your workplace, business, or facilitating things if you fail to attend to the one you need who lives in your life. Please understand beloved, you can't be so caught up that you wind up pushing your mate away causing them to get whatever they are missing somewhere else. They understand that you need to "do what you do." But also understand that they need to do some things with you as well... Don't allow yourself to stay lost living in a dark wilderness of illusion. There is definitely some give and take in the matter when your mate does not understand.

Having the career, business, and/or spot light is not all we thought it would be. Sometimes we are high-strung, all we see is what we see before us and do not bother to take a look at what is supposed to be right beside us every step of the way. We loose focus on seeing our mate right there with us as we are striving to be all that we were created to be. Driven to pursue, driven to create, driven to conquer, driven to make things happen, I must be at the top of the game. Think about it for a moment. Is what you are doing worth the real investment, which is pushing your mate further and further away because now you have become selfish, self-centered, and started to unconsciously believe that you do not need him or her. Somewhere along the way we came to the conclusion that "I can do it myself." Look at what I have already accomplished thus far. I do not need to consult with my mate, for what, so they can tell me that I should think about doing what I do a different way! Please, not me, I don't need anybody. Listen at this one people, "all I need is me." Wow! How far we have come, and for the life of us we cannot understand why our mate doesn't understand us. Trust me when I say this, doing what you love to do should not cost you your relationship with your mate if you would only communicate and include them. Give them information so they can understand. Once you've reached the point of what you defined as success, you realize you did not know it was going to cost your precious relationship with your spouse because they clearly did not understand and they most certainly did not understand you, their alleged life partner. Why are we so driven to put time, money, and electrifying energy into being the best that we can be on our jobs and in whatever else we do but fail at the really simple but important things like keeping our relationships tight with our mate? They just don't understand...

The success you were striving for is not what you thought it was going to be because you spent too much time away from home, too much time away from your friend whereas you missed out on what was really important, and that is good quality time with your mate. Since you were excessively absent mentally, emotionally, and physically, your marriage is on the rocks because you made the decision to put your vision first instead of having your partner beside you as you began to make your vision become reality. These are some of the things that happen when your mate doesn't understand. Now, I must also preface that it helps to have a mate who is completely open and comfortable in seeing you do whatever it is you do without feeling like they are in competition with you, jealous, envious, and the like as we walk out what we were created to do. We need mates who are secure in themselves who will not purposely be a hindrance to what we have a passion to do but will embrace us in our individual skills, talents, and abilities while helping to push us into our destinies. Please understand that there must be a balance and if there is not, then we need to look at this too and figure out what we need to do or how do we work through these deficiencies so that our mates get on board and ride the train alongside of us. I hope you are really taking in what I am saying to you... You need your mate to be there with you and understand the wind pushing you in your back that is causing you to move forward and pursue.

I believe what has happened over the years is that we have let society tell us what they perceived as real success. They failed to tell us that in the midst of all this pursuing our careers, expanding our businesses, and making financial growth investments that we also run a great risk of losing our mates and/or families in the name of our dream if we don't have balance. There is nothing wrong with having a dream and making it become your reality but when we achieve this dream at the expense of losing our mates, I have to stop, pause, and think for a moment. Was it really that serious? Did we really have to spend that time away? Did we really have to work all of those excessive hours without making time for the other important things in our lives? Again, these are some of the questions we need to think about for real when our mates simply just don't understand us anymore.

Having achieved the great successes ended up not being all we thought it was going to be once we got there because we did not take into account what we could possibly loose in return. It is in my opinion for us as a community of people in our own households to begin to think about how and what we are putting so much emphasis in. Having a great career and having great success is fine but we need to make sure that our mates are included into what we are doing as well. When our mates don't understand it's because we have failed to be great communicators with them, causing them to feel like they are left out in the cold, while alone not being a part of what we desire to do and be in our life. Let us not gain the whole world and in the end loose those that mean the very world to us in our pursuit of pressing towards the mark. Time and time again, we see people in Hollywood achieve what looks like success on the outside but they miss out or lose the very things that in reality were supposed to have been the most important to them.

Having your mate and being in a relationship where the lines of communication are open, while having the security of knowing you have someone who is in your corner that loves you is far more greater than just having the career or life successes alone. What good does all of it mean if at the end of the day, you don't have anyone to share it with? I hope you are getting something from what I am sharing because this reflective moment is for everyone reading my book regardless to if you are married or not. This is a life nugget I need you to digest, indeed!

We need to have a proper prospective on this thing because our mates really are very important to us. I hope that this is blessing you because it is blessing me as the Creator is giving it to me to give to you. This is something I have learned over the years of being in relationship with my husband and observing partnerships of others. Nothing should be more important to you than the well-being and healthy duality between you, your mate and/or your family. But here is the key. In order for your mate to come out of that season of not understanding you, it means that your heart needs to be sensitive to the atmosphere of where he or she are currently residing and you need to figure out what you need to do that communicates to them that they are will forever be included in whatever it is you feel you have a passion to do.

If your passion is to have the best ice cream business in town and you just won't rest until you get it, then you need to have your mate involved as you take those steps to possess your dream. If your passion is to be the best stay at home parent you can possibly be then your mate needs to be included on this and it needs to be a mutual decision between the two of you so there is no backlash in the long run. If your passion is to be president in the corporation that you are working in, then your mate needs to be included in this process so that as you go up the ladder they are coming up the ladder with you as well, which will decrease tension between the two of you because they will feel like they have been a viable contributor to your success. If your passion is to have a successful ministry, then you and your mate need to come to a mutual understanding about how the two of you will function to make the ministry a whole operate so that it does not wear out the foundation of your marriage.

I believe this is what can happen when your mate doesn't understand. In order to get rid of the strife, confusion, and tension in your marriage your mate needs and should be a part of this process. When you are pressing towards the mark and are not including them in the process, it brings division and discord into your camp. So much so that when you meet your target, you realize that it wasn't what you thought it was going to be because you lost all that was important to you in the process. Was this really, what your life was meant to be? Your precious time is now spent bitter and alone because you were too selfish to include your mate completely in your dreams. There are many in this world all alone wishing they still had their mate by their side. This is what happens when your mate doesn't understand.

Chapter 3:   When your children don't want to go

One thing I must say right at the beginning of this chapter is this. You cannot make your children go in the direction that you want them to go, period. The bible says that we as parents are to train up a child in the ways he or she should go and when they get old, they will not part from the ways which were taught to them by us.

If there were one area in my life that has been stretched tremendously, I would say that it has been in the area of raising children. I am truly an optimist and believe the very best for everyone when it comes to raising children, but trust me when I say to all of you parents out there, you cannot and I mean cannot make your children do something they clearly do not want to do themselves. Now I am speaking to you as a parent who has grown children now and let me just tell you something, at times this can be the most stressful times in your life as you are trying to raise them while also making sure you are setting an example in front of them to model after.

I have learned that the more you want for your children, the more they go against what you want! As a parent, it is not that you want to take over your children's lives but you can see the great potential they carry and push them in directions they are not interested in at all. I heard a preacher say something a few years ago in a message that just simply blew my mind and I have taken it to heart to this very day. This is what he said, "you cannot want something more for someone than they want it for themselves." Your children have got to want to go on their own, wherever that may be for their individual lives. Each child's "go" is different from yours.

The "go" for your children a lot of times is totally different from what we think their go should be. Let me repeat myself again, you cannot make your children do something that they clearly do not want to do. They must want "it" for themselves. However, in the midst of your child wanting to go his/her way, you must continue in your pursuit of being that great example that has been placed before them regardless to how much they may disappoint you. Being a parent is a very difficult job to hold sometimes because our feelings and what we think concerning our children are attached to the matters at hand when it comes to seeing them do their very best, whatever that may look like for them. Coming from a parent who understands when you see your child going down a road you think they should not be going down, while enduring the resistance from them as you try to pull them back is quite difficult and also draining. When you see your children making decisions, which you know are going to have negative long lasting results can literally feel like your inner most being is going to explode because you know they are making a huge mistake but they fight you on every hand to do what they want to do. So eventually you give in and let them...

  I have been doing this for quite some time along with my husband and I must reiterate again that your children are not going to always want to go the way you want them to go. They will do things that really disappoint you. They will display certain behaviors which have you completely baffled. They will go places they know they shouldn't be going. They will do things they know they should not do. They will test you and your authority from every side, while having you scratch your head trying to figure out what in the world just happened. Raising children can bring you to a place of utter total confusion wondering if your time invested was really worth your efforts invested.

  I think one mistake that my generation has made as

we strive to press towards the mark is learning how to effectively communicate while also actively listening to what our young people are saying to us, and also being in tune to listening to the things, which they may not be saying to us. I believe what the majority of our children are crying out for in this day and age are parents who will be parents but parents who will make themselves available to being completely involved in their children's lives. What most people in the world need and want is to know three things; feelings of being loved, needed, and feeling like they are contributing something to the world to make it a better place. From what I have observed over these last few years is a lack of parents being involved with their children completely and not making themselves available to being that listening ear when our children are crying out to us, mom/day I need you! But for whatever the reasons when they get involved in things we don't understand or make mistakes, which take us aback we have the nerve to say, I don't know what in the world got into Sally or Tom... Do you understand the message I am trying to relay to you reader? If you have children whom you are raising and they don't want to go, you need to ask yourself why? I am in no way blaming you as a parent at all for whatever your son or daughter has gotten off into but what I am saying is that we do have a certain amount of influence over our children if we make them feel like they are important to us and show a genuine concern along with showering unconditional love upon them. You cannot just tell your child not to do something because you said so because in this day and age they want to know why but you must give them a visual so they can understand why you are so passionate about them not making the wrong decisions in life or going down roads we really want them to make a u-turn on. In this day and age we as parents tend to make ourselves so busy and forget about going to the simple things of life which make life what it is, sweet. We need to go back to the basics. Sit down after you get home from work and talk to your children about how their day went. Ask them if there are things going on that they need to talk. Be open to hearing and listening to your child express their feelings on whatever subject or topic they bring up without butting in like we as parents oftentimes do. Listen sometimes to your child when they speak with attentive ears to hear with your heart as well because you just might learn something you never knew about them. Now I will preface this comment by saying that you may not always agree with how they think or view a particular topic in their lives but just listen. You don't always have to chime in on everything they say at those moments because you need to get to know your child as they begin to evolve into being the young man or woman that used to be your "baby." They are not a baby anymore. You now have someone living with you who has a mind of their own and who may not share the same thoughts and views as you do, that is why you need to listen sometimes and not always speak. Take some mental notes and come back to address whatever you need to address at a later time. It's called relationship and that is what our children are crying out for from us as parents. They need someone who will be a parent to them and not a friend but someone they really can share their thoughts with or talk to about whatever is bothering them. They are not on the receiving end of this type of treatment from us and this is why they don't want to go the way we want them to go.

I hope you are getting something from this insight being shared with you because it has caused me many sleepless nights, tears cried, arguments, and putting people to flight to pass this information on to you in hopes that you the reader, putting it to good use. I am the first partaker of what I am giving to you and trust me, what I am saying to you really works. Believe that. Ask my children. How about this, test what I said, put it into action and see what happens between you and your son(s) or daughter(s). A relationship will begin to evolve and you will begin to understand, learn, and most of all love your children in an even more beautiful way because you will realize that what you see in them is so precious, and how you need to do everything in your power to embrace them so that you as a parent can help push them into their own destiny.

I originally wrote this book three years ago in July of two thousand eight and then picked this manuscript back up in July of 2011. What I originally wrote in this chapter has completely changed. Most of what I wrote has been deleted because I needed to learn so more things when it comes to this subject matter of rearing children before I offered some reflecting thoughts to you. I obviously needed to learn some new things which would impact and empower you because there are many of you right now that are experiencing in your lives with your children the experience of "they don't want to go." You really need to think about this and figure out why they don't won't to go (the way you want them to go) then ask them through open and honest dialogue where they want to go (find out what they think and what makes them tick). As a parent you can't always think that what you want for your child is the best thing for them. Sure your intentions are genuine but your child may be totally rebelling on the inside because you are trying to force a lifestyle on them that they are not interested in pursuing let alone living.

Now I also want to add balance to what I am saying to you as well. We want to provide our children with the opportunity at times to make their own decisions when it comes to living their lives; however that does not mean that we give them the authority to under mind our role as being parents to them along the way. We still require they give us our respect because we are their parent. They will not talk to us crazy. They will not try to harm us physically. They will not disrespect us in any way, why? Because we demand it! We still will tell them about themselves when they are flat out wrong. We will console them as they need it. And we will comfort them when they are going through something. So just because we have taken on a different plan of action doesn't mean we give them the opportunity to treat us any different, we are still their parents and that is the bottom line... We can still afford them the opportunities of having options but that does not mean we as parents will lower our standards by any measure. When there is no standard we allow any and everything to take place under the roofs of our houses. Shame on us if this is what we have allowed to happen and then we still have the nerve to say I don't understand why they don't want to go. We must lift up the standards in our homes, our children are crying out for it. They need structure. They need guidance. They need wisdom imparted to them by their parents. Simply said, they need you.

I will also be realistic as well to some degree because I have shared real information with you my readers thus far. In this season of life I see many young people telling their parent or parents what they will and will not do and have some of us running scared or for cover and I think that is absolutely ridiculous but that is another subject indeed. So don't get mad when they don't want to go where you want them to go or do what you want them to do. Just hope that the foundation you laid before them is strong and secure being able to hold them regardless of the things they say and do. The hope is that as they grow older they will not depart from the things you taught them (if they were good things) which were truly foundational in their lives. The only question I have to ask you as a parent to another parent is what type of foundation did you lay before them. Is it a foundation of truth, meaning that you lived out what you were telling them? Or is the foundation shaky? You talked a lot but you really were not saying anything. They (your children) watched you and said you were full of it. You don't practice anything that you preach. They say you were a big hypocrite and I refuse to "go" anywhere you have been.

When we were coming up, our parent (s) gave us spankings and it didn't hurt us. We turned out great. We respected our parents no matter how much we didn't like what they were telling us. We totally acknowledged them as our parents and never got that role confused or crossed the boundaries. We didn't understand why they were so hard nor did we understand the things they did when it came to raising us but they were trying to do the best they could. They loved us and simply wanted the best for us. Now they may not have been the best communicator with us nor catered to our every need but they tried the best way they could even though we may feel it wasn't their best and they could have done a whole lot more and then some.

Since some of us chose to be very lax in raising our children, we can't get upset with them if they don't want to go in the direction that you want them to go in. But that still should not stop you from pointing things out to them because they have to learn to think things through. Our young people in this hour only live for the moment and the day. They don't believe they have a future or a purpose. Why do they feel this way? It is in my opinion, due to many parents across the board being lax with their own lives and selves, they believe there is not a point to pressing ahead and achieving in theirs. We must give them a reason to hope. They must be able to see through us that because of hope mom or dad pressed forward and made it happen in spite of all the odds, which may have been against them.

It is my desire that this chapter be one

encouragement to all the parents who feel like they are struggling and at their wits end but you have this book in your hands and now understand that you are not in this by yourself. You need to know that for me, this is a heart matter because I really want to see you be all that you can be as you press towards the mark and your children have shown you that they do not want to go, period!. I am not by any means downplaying the difficult, challenging, and oh so rewarding job of being a parent. I am simply stating that you as a mother or father cannot get frustrated when your children don't go the way you think they should go. I strongly believe that two of the biggest things our children need from us is to love them first and then second accept them totally, the good along with the bad. I mean remember I just covered that topic thoroughly with you in chapter one of this book. Let me be the first to tell you first hand that that can be frustrating and/or disappointing at times, but they are our babies and this is all that we have for our future so why not make the best of the situation and love your children for who they are as a unique person even if they don't want to go the way you want them to go or live the way we think they should live.

Be patient because your labor of love was not in vain. You will reap a great harvest with your children if you are not weak and do not faint. It is always darkest before dawn. Just when you think that things can't get any worst, they sometimes do. However, you need to remember that in regards to your babies, weeping may endure for a night but your joy is coming in the morning time. You just got to keep fighting for your kids in prayer and telling the enemy that he can't have them because they belong to God.

Let me share a thought with you. I have talked to many parents who have teenagers and I find it amazing the things we are coming up against when it comes to our children. It seems as though parents are having a universal challenge. The language, the ups, the downs, the hi's, and the lo's all the same. Parents are crying out with the same language and the youth are saying the same thing in regards to us. The youth are saying that their parents just don't understand them, we don't know how to relate to them, we are too old, and we are never around because we have to work, or we always have too many things to do. And remember I just talked about this a little bit in chapter two that pursuing careers without communication with our families can put us in jeopardy of losing our families. So here again, I have to ask a question for you to think about. Is all that you are doing really worth the livelihood of your household, your children?

It's ok to pursue things you feel will make your family better off but I want you to think about how dedicated you are versus how dedicated you are to spending time and being around for the well-being of your children? They are so precious and they mean the world to us, they really do. Listen, I know most of us mean well but see this is a trick of the enemy to have us so busy that we wind up losing our families. We have lost our men as solid fathers in the children's lives. Our men cover and affirm who they are and where they come from, while our mothers job is to nurture and care for them. We have lost our son's and our daughters to other people who are influencing our children into wild self-destructive behaviors. We have lost them to friends in the streets or other places of solace for them who they feel more of a connection with than their own parents. How backwards have things become? This is an example of the decay of the family which has already taken place over the past few years. If you don't believe me, all you have to do is open your eyes and look right around you. Observe and explore what I am saying to you. It is true.

Let's consider something as simple as this. If you are a family of any size, number doesn't matter in this case I just want you tothink about it. When was the last time your family sat down together at the dinner table and had dinner together as a family or breakfast for that matter? I am talking about turning the television off, everybody off the telephone, everybody at home at the same time and just sitting down together as family breaking bread together. You see, it is simple things like this that have become uncommon in most of our homes which are supposed to be common. We don't spend time with each other and we see each other in passing. Today dinner is usually everyone eating at different times of the evening. And even in that case we are not even eating in the dining room or in the kitchen area. We are spending that precious time eating in front of the television, in front of the computer, or while we are making some kind of business deal over the telephone. We have simply begun to lose the strength of what it really means to be a family.

Now I could present you with a lot of facts and statistics, however I speaking to you in a manner throughout this book where it is my hope that the thoughts I share become a topic(s) of discussion generating dialogue within your own households and communities. Think of me right now as one of your close friends who you are talking to and confiding in. Let me let you in on something, I am no different from anybody reading this book. I have been just as guilty as the next person but I think what the Creator is allowing me to do now is to begin to share some things with you we have experienced because we are not the only ones walking through these hardships in raising children as we press towards the mark for a higher prize. We have become enlightened and finally have figured out what the key is that unlocks the door to the heart of our children. It is us. It is you my friend.

It is my desire in this project to bring some type of internal awareness because we had to changed and we needed to come back to what was really most important. We had pressed toward a mark but the mark that we received was really hard pill to swallow. Did we mean to latch on to things we thought were important and in turn it was revealed through all these many years that we had only deceived our own selves? We had been believing and living a lie that we thought was our own personal truth. I just want to present some thoughts to you to take into consideration and cause you to pause for a minute and reflect.

It is time to stop being fake, phony, and acting like we really have it all together in front of our children when we know in our heart that we don't but we want them to listen to us… Yeah right! Guess what the biggest outcome of this is? Our children are watching us and they feel like, "I ain't doin all that stuff I seen my mom or my dad do." They feel like for what, so that they can feel all the stress and tension that we do due to not knowing who you are because you are have been suffering from an acute case of identity crisis. They see and experience us being touchy, snappy, and moody all the time, which makes them pull away. We have become to them in irrelevant to them an extreme degree. This is why in my opinion they feel closer to their friends outside of the home than they do with us, their own flesh and blood. Listen beloved, this assignment I have been given is to be straight up with you. I am not trying to preach to you but I am talking to you from my heart and telling you that it is time for us as parents to wake up and see the handwriting on the wall. Our children refuse to go where we want them to go or do the things we want them to do because they feel like their efforts in that thing would be futile and we are a huge part of their perception of where and what they see for themselves.

I need to make this clear. I will repeat this again because I need this to get into your spirit. I am not saying that we have to lower our standards when it comes to our young people because we don't. However, there must be a standard that is raised by you and it must be met in some type of way with a healthy balance. We must somehow give our children or show them in some type of form that there is more to their life than what they may be currently experiencing. They need to feel like there is hope. They need to feel like they are wanted. They need to feel like they mean something to us. Most of all they need to feel like they are loved. The bible shares the thought that love covers a multitude of sins. When we love on our kids they will begin to feel like they are significant and that they are somebody most of all to us, their parents.

Think on that beloved because we need our kids, they are our definite future. Without them, there is no us. Let us give them a reason to come and follow us in the way that they are supposed to for themselves so that they will "go" places they have always dreamed about while making us proud and happy parents in the process because they now have a strong desire which pushes them to finally "go."

Chapter 4:   When you are single & trying to stay strong

I will tell you the plain ole absolute truth and not lie, being single and trying to stay strong is hard. Now don't get me wrong, it has its advantages but it also has its frustrations as well. One of the biggest things one seems to enjoy in their singleness is being able to come and go as you please. There is no one in your life you have to answer too and no one is asking you questions concerning where you have been and who you went there with. How about that, must be nice huh? Well my friend I must admit to a certain degree it is.

I believe in your singleness you go through seasons of growing and learning about who you are as a man or woman and figuring out what you want out of life along with also coming to definitive answers about what you think you would like to accomplish in your life. You also go through tough places of loneliness as well. Sure you are beautifully single and loving it for the time being but let's be real, sometimes you feel alone and lonely all at the same time. You can hardly get the weight off you at times. Your mind, body, and soul craves for the attention you feel you need in those moments of your life. You have feelings, wants, and desires running through you and you really just want someone to come along and take care of your most intimate needs. You are lonely but yet you are trying to press towards the mark while doing your absolute best to stay strong. Sometimes you wonder if you are going to ever make it through or if there will ever be anyone who will come along and simply sweep you off your feet so you do not have to bare the pain of this burden anymore. Your mind is craving for intellectual stimulation. Your soul is longing for that emotional connection which attaches itself to that which gives you hope. Your body is yearning to be kissed, touched, hugged, and you know... You ask yourself time and time again, what am I going to do? I can't take this anymore; I got to "get me some!" You say to yourself, "no I can't do that." I need to wait. Then you ask yourself what is the point in all of this waiting and why do I really need to wait? Being single and trying to stay strong can sometimes feel like you are ripping yourself in pieces because of your needs, wants, and desires that you want fulfilled right now and you are tired of waiting! Then someone comes along and you begin to think is this the one but really it isn't. The fact of the matter is you are full of lust and completely horny so you begin to contemplate should I do something with this person or should I wait.

We are all adults reading this book and I am not going to sugarcoat this topic or any for that matter, so do not act like you are in shock by what I have already said and what I am about to say now. People in their singleness are not waiting anymore until they get married. They are having sex right now and have no thoughts about waiting. People are getting the sexual gratification which they have been longing for. People are seeking to get their needs met. Now does that mean because they are "doing it" that it is the right thing for one to do under these circumstances? I do not think so but the fact of the matter is, people are in this place in their lives and they are carrying out certain thoughts they are having. My perspective is not to judge you at all because I have been there but as a personal development specialist/life coach, my job now is to get you think about why you do the things you do. And if the decisions you are making are detrimental to your internal and mental health, why do you or "we" continue to do the same things over and over, which keep us in bondage? Now, I realize the society we are living in condones premarital sex, living together, and common-law marriages, "right?" But I must tell you that you are worth so much more and that you are selling yourself short when you accept these things for your life. Trying before you buy does not always pan out as we thought it would and neither does giving in so that you can fulfill your sexual needs. Let me preface my statement; it is easier said than done I know because again we are talking about being single and trying to stay strong as you press towards your mark. So as your coach I must ask, in the context of this topic what do you desire in your singleness? What is your personal preference? What is the acceptable mark for you? Nobody really thinks about these types of questions for real because if you did we wouldn't be giving ourselves away to everyone who comes along and makes us feel good with certain words or for the simple fact the they look good (physically), which oftentimes causes us to give in to "giving them some." It seems as though everything has been permitted to be acceptable in our society.

It is in my opinion that we have more problems in our lives as a single person because we have made conscientious decisions to lower our standards of living and our own personal morals. Having sex with anyone you feel like is commonplace now. What happened to really getting to know someone and developing a relationship as friends first and not friends with benefits? Do you understand? We have become *doggish* in our thinking and we give ourselves away sexually to any and everybody when the gift of us should be just that, a gift to whoever our husband or wife is going to be. Remember, we are talking about being single and trying to stay strong folks.

Then I think one of the other pressures we have is now we are driven to always be by our self. We have this mentality in our world that says I don't need a woman or I don't need a man. I can make it on my won. Well beloved, I beg to differ. We all need someone special that aids in bringing more beauty into our lives and also bring more of the beauty within us out. This thought is foolish to me because a few years ago I felt the same way. After I came out of a horrible first marriage to the father of my two oldest children, I took on that mentality for a while where I said "I don't need a man, I have a good job, and it will just be me and my kids from here on out." That is what I said then. Sure, I was doing ok for myself at that time. I had all the freedom in the world to do whatever I wanted to do whenever I wanted to do it. I didn't have to answer for any decisions that I made. I took care of business, which was my household, my children, and myself and felt like I was doing just fine. However, what I began to understand about myself is that I was being selfish. I am a great person to be around so why would I limit myself and say that I would never ever consider being in a relationship with someone that I looked at as husband material again. I knew somewhere along the way that there was a man out there who was looking for the gift of me and felt like they needed me.

I believe in this society that we live in our thinking has become polluted and warped to believe that it will always be this sarcastic description of the me, myself, and I mentality. It is in my opinion that it is hard to stay strong or true to that way or thinking or that philosophy. Just take a look around you at those that have been single for years who really are lonely and wish that they had someone in their life on a more permanent basis simply to just share life with. How about that? We all need somebody and there is somebody that needs us too. I just want to keep it real with you. Being single is nice and has some temporary advantages but it is not the way to go for the rest of your days on this earth. At some point and time your heart should become un-hardened and pliable to the ways of thinking that says yes, one day I am going to get married, I am going to stop sleeping around, I will keep myself for whoever my mate is because I deserve that and so do they. Or how about this, when you and your potential life partner are talking and really getting to know each other in a very real way sharing all of your "business" and have to reveal to each other how many sex partners you've had... How will you feel if you must say that the number of people you slept with is some outstanding number. When you think about it if that is your truth or you once were in a relationship with someone and that was their truth, how did that cloud your thinking of that person? Let's just be real beloved. You don't think very highly of those who have had a lot of sexual partners because in this day and age you know firsthand this will have or can have some type of effect on you not only mentally but physically as well, especially if that person was not consistently protecting themselves with each sexual partner. I must challenge you here as you move forward in pressing towards the mark because this is your life and for me this is serious business when it comes to you! I must challenge you as your personal development specialist because I need you to learn how to cherish yourself and practice some self-control because those fifteen or twenty minutes of ecstasy is not worth the rest of your life with sicknesses and disease. You are beautiful. You are valuable. You are a priceless commodity. And you deserve so much more than what your current being single experience may be. Do you understand what I am saying to you?

In our younger year's we want to be single and that is just how it is. We don't care about what anyone has to say about what we do or how we choose to do it when we want to do it. As a matter of fact, I believe we should celebrate life and all that it has to offer as a single person and enjoy it. Those are your formative years as an adult and you need that time to discover who you are as young woman or young man. I personally am not really all that fond of people getting into serious relationships right after graduating high school, in college, or even after you graduate college because I think you are way too young and haven't given yourself time to begin to know and understand you first. Also to add to it you do not know what you want or expect out of life let alone a life partner.

I think if you are tied down pre-maturely, it does have a possibility of stagnating you, your growth, and development. You may ask why I say that. Well I will share a little of my experience. I first got married when I was twenty years old and had my first child as well. I got pregnant before the marriage obviously but we thought and were told that we should get married because that was the right thing to do. Well let me just tell you that was not the right thing to do. It was the wrong thing to do. As a matter of fact, it was one of the biggest mistakes that I could've made at such a early time in my life. First of all, I didn't really know this person like I thought I did. Second of all, I did not allow myself to experience life as a young woman before I got into this major commitment. Thirdly, to really bring all of this grown up stuff home, I had a little baby that I had to think about as well. Fourthly, I just was not ready for something like that mentally, physically, or spiritually because I did not even know who I was as a young budding woman at the time. I simply settled for anything and because I settled, I endured seven years of hell for not listening to that inner voice trying to warn me not to do it.

Now I realize that my experience could be different than yours but the point is this a reality for some when you are single and trying to stay strong. When you are young and single, you take on this mentality that you know it all and you have it together. This is perfectly fine, trust me it is. However, this is what I need you to wrap your mind around as we grow in life and discover who we are, we become grounded in whatever is our worldview, our morals, or standards in life are. There comes a time in all of our lives in our singleness where we all must go back and review some things. Then we need to take a self-evaluation or self-assessment of ourselves and figure out what in our life is really important and then decide to take action to get rid of the things which are not as important as we may have initially thought.

You see my friend being single and trying to stay strong as you press towards the mark can get a little tricky when we make permanent decisions in temporary circumstances. We must learn to shut people and relationships off in our lives because we are changing and beginning to figure out who we are and what we are supposed to be doing with our lives. In your singleness, you don't want to wake up one day and discover that in your being single and trying to stay strong that it was not what you thought it was going to be due to poor decisions affecting you in the long run. You are single true enough but now you might me miserable, bitter, and just a nasty person to be around. Now this may not be the scenario for most but I am trying to give you an different examples of people I personally know who fit into these categories. Being single and trying to stay strong is really not all that it is cracked up to be.

I suggest to you that while you are single make the most of your life in that season. Enjoy everything that it brings you, good and bad. Glean off every circumstance, adversity, and triumph that you go through for it is preparing you for your bright future. You don't want be single always true enough, but while you are, make sure that a good foundation is being laid on your behalf because you are worth that much.

Now I know there may be a lot of books and

materials out on the market teaching you strategies and the like on being single, and they may have very good information for you to follow. However, it is my opinion that life is sometimes your best teacher and it is good to follow your instincts. Most of the times when you do that you don't go wrong. Therefore, being single and staying strong has its ups and its downs but the point I believe God is impressing upon me to tell you is not to put yourself in a box or compromising circumstances that will have long term negative effects. When you choose to live that way limitations are placed on you because you put these unrealistic ideas in your head that you have all the answers and that you don't need anyone because you can take care of you and that you don't need nobody. You also determined for yourself that you can sleep with anyone you wanted whenever you wanted to. Sure, that is a fine attitude to take but eventually you do need someone special to share your life, time, and space with. There is someone destined for you.

Don't shun the idea of marriage. Please don't think it is just something to do and then when you get tired you get a divorce. There are many, many marriages like that in America in shambles but in the context of what I am discussing with you in this context is you can have someone in your life and it can be a wonderful relationship that the two of you work on together so it lasts. I didn't mean to get on this subject totally about marriage but I feel the need to enlighten my single and my married audience on a couple of things. Making a decision to get married and stay married is not all based on your feeling of "you love them." It is based on the foundational principle which you promised to stay committed to. This covenant agreement was made before your God and in front of all those who were witnesses at your ceremony. Marriage is something the two of you have to work on continually every day. The second thing that I need to say is that when you make the decision to get married you must realize you will re-learn yourself all over again now that you are in a marriage. It is a give and take. Nevertheless, it must be something the two of you agree to do and happens the very day that the two of you say, "I do."

I believe these two things I mentioned are important because most people get married with the idea it is going to be just like peaches and cream when that is far from the truth. Your being single and trying to staying strong cannot enter into the relationship because it can have a strong possibility of sabotaging the relationship if you do not get a grasp on your independence. I hope you understand what I am sharing with you. You can have this thought that says "who the hell are you (your mate)?" I don't have to listen to you. I've been living like this for however many years that you have been single and I am not going to change for you or nobody else for that matter. Honey, let me tell you that is wrong, wrong, wrong! You made a covenant agreement to work things out I don't care how bad you feel like it's getting. Now let just pause right here because there will some who will experience abusive type issues and I am not condoning that whatsoever and saying you must stay because you shouldn't. If one you cheated on the other it is up to you accordingly to try to work things out should you choose to do that but the decision is yours. By all means do what you believe is the best thing for you. Outside of that I am optimistic in believing that two people who honestly love each other unconditionally can work things out in their marriage but it takes two! Not one but two! Both parties have to want it for it to work.

Currently, we have a lot of poor examples of marriage and it looks like a joke at times. So consequently you have many who don't believe in marriage anymore or esteem it highly. The couples who have been guilty of painting this picture for us don't realize the seriousness of what they vowed to do and how it has affected those who were watching them. To my single women who will one day get married. Please don't put unrealistic burdens on the man you will one day marry. If he is working and doing what he needs to do to take care of business then you celebrate him and let him know how much you appreciate him. If he doesn't have a house, so what. If all he has is an apartment, it's a start for a brighter tomorrow for the two of you but he needs you to encourage him in all that he does. The woman builds her man up by embracing all the good that she sees in him. Please understand that. We have gotten some very poor teaching if any on a real relationship in a real marriage in a real world. To my brothers out there, show your wives that you love them by telling them that you love them and embracing them in who they are as a woman. A woman needs to know that she is your heart. Support each other in the decisions you each will make for your lives. Learn to make yourselves available to understand each other as well. Most of all men spend excellent quality time with your lady then she will know that you really do care about her and that honestly you do love her.

It is my prayer that this chapter right here really blesses you as you read it because I really believe in my heart that this information shared is highly important. Not only from a single persons point of view but it helps to prepare you so that while you are in the dating scene you have some type of measuring rod to use that will help guide you along the way when it comes to dealing with the opposite sex.

You can be single and you can try to stay strong but I feel like you must have a balance in all things. You don't want to come off to strong where no one would ever consider approaching you and then you don't want to come off as an arrogant snob who thinks they are all that and a bag of chips. You also do not want to come across as an airhead with signals saying that anything goes. Nor do you want to come across as one who is desperate and will except anything. Do you understand what I am getting at? Be patient, your time will come. Save your goodies for that special one designed just for y-o-u. Stop selling yourself short because you are priceless and worth so much more than the person you have had on display in your present state of being single. It all goes back to knowing who you are in your quest for pressing toward the mark.

Chapter 5:   When your family does not support you

So many times in life, we have passions that are driving us or things that we need or want to accomplish and our family is sitting on the sidelines looking us complaining about what they see us doing. It seems like all you do never matches up or lines up to their expectations. Listen beloved, I know that most our families may mean well but sometimes they knowingly or unknowingly hurt us when they do not support whatever it is, which drives us.

How do you handle the scandal? How do you handle the scrutiny? How does one handle being talked about by those who we thought would be our biggest supporters? How do you handle the lies told about you? How do you handle being the outcast? These questions to name a few are only some examples to give you and let you see how your families can mistreat when you decide that you will go after your dreams in spite of and press towards the mark. They do not understand that you have been chosen to be different from most people. You have been handpicked for a specific reason. You are not average whatsoever, regardless of what your family may think or say. In fact, there is a reason as to why you have an entrepreneurial spirit within you. You always got along well in life not being a part of the "family mess." That was always something you never took pleasure in. As a matter of fact you hated hearing your family talk about everyone while forgetting to look at themselves in their own delusions. Life is tricky enough as it is to maneuver through but when you add the dynamic of being surrounded by an unsupportive family that alone takes you and what you desire to do to a whole other level of chaos and despair. Just when you think they are possibly on the team, usually something always goes wrong!

You have made decisions to do things nobody in
your family has ever done before and it does not matter to
you what price you will have to pay to do that which is
driving you. Here is an example to illustrate what I am
sharing with you. Jesus said over in the book of Matthew
that if anyone wanted to follow him they must first take up
their cross and follow him. You have to carry that weight
like he did and it get very hard as you begin to take a long
journey through your life like he did. The Creator himself
handpicked picked little old you out of your ordinary life to
do something extraordinary that would literally change
lives while altering the course of those headed in the wrong
direction headed to destination nowhere or dead end. The
dream you have is a dream which causes friction where
people think you feel like you are better than them. They
even entertain conversations and ask questions amongst
themselves as to why you pulled away from them. There is
a great answer to bring clarity to all of their questions. You
dared not only to dream big but you took a huge gamble
and you stepped out of your comfort zone to make your
dream become your reality!

This does not mean that you think you are better
them but you simply have a desire to do something that
truly makes a difference instead of standing on the sideline
of life watching others making a difference. Families have
a hard time dealing with creative people sometimes because
we are not afraid to step over the boundary lines of the
norm. We are not afraid to take risks. We are risky people.
We feel like we don't have anything to loose, while
knowing, we have everything to gain. However, our
families don't understand and they don't support us in some
of the decisions we chose to make good, bad, or indifferent.
Do I have any witnesses out there?

Now, let me preface beloved, I am not trying to
come off like a know-it-all because I am not but I am just

giving it to you real straight with no chaser. This is the real world and this is how it can oftentimes be with your own family because quite simply put, they do not believe in you. You would think you would deal with this type of behavior with your friends before your family but that is not always the case. Now I realize also this is may not be the case for minority, the 20% but for those who are coming up the ranks over in the 80%, these folks are fighting hard to make their "it" happen! There could possibly be some exceptions to what I've shared but it is my opinion and you do not have to agree. Again remember I said earlier in the book how much I desire for you the reader to take some of the topics shared throughout this book and begin to dialogue and have discussions about what I share and then determine for yourself where you are or define what you think. It is funny how your family most times will not support you at first but if what you are doing opens up opportunities, which lead to success then you will hear things like, "I always knew that you were special, or I always knew you were going to be successful and make something of yourself." Isn't that crazy? This is when you get all types of support from them but when you were coming up on the rough side of the mountain, you couldn't get any kind of help at all.

Dealing with family can be a trip with an uncertain destination but you just simply learn how to deal and you learn how to cope because your future looks so much brighter than your past and what you may currently be experiencing when it comes to your passion in what you are doing to make a huge impact in the world. When you step out and do things your family does not understand, it tends to be frustrating in the context of you clearly understanding why you do what you do, whatever that is. It is your driving force but your family members cannot see what you see. This is what causes many families to lose touch with visionaries or creative people like yourself because they have been so used to be normal and average instead of embracing extraordinary, which is who you are. But what do you do when you know that you have not been put in this earth to be normal carry out normal things. I am not average and neither are you who are reading my book!

What do you do with family that cannot understand your passion? You have tried talking to them, befriending them, but nothing simply seems to be working. Therefore, the effect of what you will have to deal with is this… You have these feelings of being ostracized, persecuted, forsaken, and just flat out abused. Nobody understands the song you are singing. However, it does not matter to you anymore what they think or even what they say because you are determined in your mind that you will make it, you will succeed, and there is nothing that anyone can do to keep you away from fulfilling your purpose. So you will have a season my friend where you will have to pull away or distance yourself from certain family members who are guilty of being a purpose and dream killer!

I hope that somebody is getting something out of what I am sharing here with you in. You can make it even when your family does not support you in the decisions that you have made. Having your family follow you is not something easy for them to do. For example, if you are a baby sister in your family and you are doing well, your siblings may feel like they do not have to listen to you or follow your lead because you are the baby but really you are functioning as the eldest child. This type of behavior brings strife, discord, and offense. Beware because when this type of behavior creeps in it can be like cancer, it will spread like wildfire, which is hard to keep under control if not stopped right when it first begins.

It is hard for the family to accept the blatant fact of you not being the average person but are a leader who leads. Keep in mind there is something in you that you have been created to do, you must give it to the world, and you must accomplish everything you set out to do while sometimes making costly mistakes along the way. Your journey can and will be a difficult one at full of hardship, good times, major triumphs, and sometimes sprinkled with despair but whatever it is that you must endure to get there to your "it" as you press towards the mark, tell yourself in all situations be it good or bad that I will persist until I succeed regardless if my family is there or not there supporting me!

The bottom line is this, it doesn't matter what your family says or thinks. They are not the influential factor in you making a tangible impact in the world so that you will one leave a living legacy for others to be blessed and inspired from. You have a goals set before you to accomplish. What are you going to do? Are you going to sit on it because your family does not accept it? Or are you going to proceed forward and change the world by doing what is in you to do. These are some of the challenges you are faced with when your family does not understand.

Chapter 6:   When it seems like nothing is working

Pressing towards the mark when it seems as though nothing is working can make you to feel like you are losing your mind! You will find yourself many times questioning why you are doing whatever it is you are doing. You will also look within and try to rationalize or determine what the real motives were for you moving forward with this thing you desire to do while not seeing any return whatsoever, so you think!

It is in these times where you as a person are really defined and you also come face-to-face with the real you because of the pressure being applied to you and your life. You feel like you are the craziest person in the world daring to go where no one you know has ever gone before. Pressing forward when it seems like when you view your circumstances with your human eye are absolutely null and your efforts spent are void and availing you absolutely nothing... Many of you who are reading my book are called in to do some extraordinary things that will literally change the world, re-shape how people think, and challenge the intelligent in ways they have not even fathomed as I write these words to you now.

It is in these moments when it seems as though nothing is working when you have to dig down even deeper within yourself and push even more. I know you don't feel like it. I know you are tired and want to stop but you cannot give up because you live, breath, and eat what you were created to do and I know beyond a shadow of a doubt somebody needs what you have to give to them! Do I have any witnesses? I am convinced I do because when it got tight for me these were some of the things I experienced as well and a whole lot more.

These times in your life are very trying indeed and you almost feel like it is way too hard for you to accomplish what you set out to do. There were many road blocks to overcome as you began your travels. There were many mountains you've had to climb up. There were numerous barriers which were always presenting themselves to you every time you felt like you were making some headway. Look at all of those times you had to stay down in the valley of despair while trying to keep that beautiful smile on your face as you tried to convince others "all is well." There were always questions of can I really do this? How can I do this? Where is the money going to come from so that I can do this? Who is going to support me? Where are my financial backers to invest in my vision? I know this will work, it's got to work! This is what happens when it seems as though none of your efforts are bringing forth the outcomes you intended or envisioned.

What do you do and where do you go from here? What is your next step? Do you have to revise your plan of action? Do you need to re-align yourself with the different people who were not in your circle of influence? Or do you keep on doing it the way you originally thought you were supposed to? My friend this is such a hard and difficult place to be in because you are now in the valley of decision for some and for others it may feel like you are in the valley of despair. Where do you go? Who do you see? Am I really going crazy? This doesn't make sense. Is this really even realistic? What am I going to do now? When it seems like nothing is working in your favor the first impulse is to throw your hands up and say I can't do this anymore and I quit. You have no hope and cannot see the light at the end of the tunnel but you cannot see yourself giving up on your dream, your vision, your plan… What do you do? Do you go back to a life of what others call normalcy? Sometimes you have to sit for a moment and it could be a long moment and think about what you have just done and gotten yourself into. You know that you are in deep. I want you to ask yourself probing questions, which will help you get to the root of whatever your outcomes were and also help you to deal with how you feel. Make sure you are connected to the right people who can help you through these trying times. Make sure your circle of influence is a mixture of those who have "been there done that already" folks, aspiring to achieve in their area folks, connector folks (those who know somebody that knows somebody), challenger folks (those who believe in your dream but ask you the hard questions), and then the folks that actually just give a damn about you. You need all of these people because wherever your destination is supposed to take you on your road to greatness, you can't get their by yourself. You need these all of these people in your life.

It is in these moments that we sometimes have to go back to the drawing board and rearrange some things in the plan, even tweaking it a little more, which can make it better. You come to realize that in spite of all of the hardships it is all to the good because even when we make think in those moments that all of our efforts were in vain, it turns out that they really were not. Our idea was brilliant but it needed to be thought out even more. Our plan was a great plan but we needed to be stretched in our capacity of thinking a little more. We really could get our businesses up and going but we needed to dream bigger. Listen, there were many and are many lessons you learn, which no one can teach you. These are priceless lessons that make you wiser and smarter for the long haul of your journey as you are pressing towards the mark. You are gaining a new and better perspective.

It is in these times where we have become the most fertile and grow. In our brokenness of feeling like we are not making any headway we are able to see ourselves in a

different light as well. We are getting some much needed
fine tuning. I have determined more than likely you will
get more clarity of your vision in these somber moments of
your life because you are little more open to listen to the
voice of reason, wisdom, and insight from others who
believe in you and want to impart into you, but before they
couldn't get to you because you had all the answers as well
all of the right moves in your moment of creativity for your
dream. Now you are open to listen and as you listen, you
begin to understand how you could been more effective in
your approach. You understand your delivery when you
were conveying the message of your visions could have
been a little clearer. You understand that even when you
thought you were communicating effectively, you know
now you really weren't because your audience totally
missed the message you wanted to convey to them. Am I
making sense? I really hope this is helping you (all of my
readers)!

We need these moments, every last one of them
because they make us so much better. They cause us to
really sharpen up on our craft to the point we deliver it with
extreme excellence no matter what "it" is. There are no
questions now about what we are saying or what our
message is because we are communicating in a more
effective manner. Our audience is now drawn to us as soon
we open our mouths or do whatever it is that we do. We
couldn't have gotten this way if things did not seem like
they were working as we pressed toward the mark.

So my dear friends don't beat yourselves up to bad.
You need these moments in your quest. These moments
design, form, and shape you into being. They can make you
and they oftentimes can break you in a much needed way.
Don't be discouraged and please do not despair. Come out
of your depression and anxiety now! Relax, take a deep
breath my friend, and breathe out slowly. You are going to

make because I said you have no other choice to make it.
This is the secret behind-the-scenes with you because
nobody knows when they see you that there is a real
struggle going on from within you. When they see you, all
they see and experience is that this person who is doing
whatever it is they do seamlessly. It appears to them that all
of your ducks are in a row. You look like success. You act
like success. And you are saying to yourself, if they only
knew the struggle. Let me affirm what your feeling or
emotions you could be experiencing at this very moment as
you are reading my book, understand I truly believe that
they are real and I acknowledge it taking place in your life
as I speak to you. However, I am charged to give you this
information because I know it will give you some insight as
to why you feel what you feel and how you can you're your
way through it to get yourself back on top. I want you to
begin to feel a whole lot better about yourself and your call
in this life to carry out and accomplish. When it seems as
though nothing you are doing is working please believe that
it really is. You have already touched so many people who
you were not even aware of watching your every step. And
because you did your thing with excellence they made it a
little bit further in life. So give yourself a handclap for
accomplishing that great feat my friend while you feel as
though nothing you do matters…

Chapter 7:   When you find your strength

Perhaps this will be the most important chapter I write to you as we bring this book to a close. Finding your strength as you are pressing toward the mark will be essential to your personal success and healthy personal development so that as you achieve your successes. You will have a clearer perspective which makes better sense to you causing your life to be in order with having a clear defined identity of who you are along with defining your purpose, relationships intact and proper order, Having a mate who is happy to be with you walking along side of you, and most importantly you are healthy mentally, spiritually, and physically. This is key for you as because as you can already see as you have begun to reflect throughout this book, "it is not what you think." Pressing towards the mark is about finding that place within the very core of your being called your soul where you find inner peace. A peace that is very sweet. It is a peace where you find the happiness you need, which helps you survive and live each and every day to the fullest.

When you find your strength it means that you have begun to process, while becoming illuminated to the things that keep you on tract and more sensitive to that which you must tear away so that you do not stay distracted and off course with aligning to your destination. Pressing towards the mark should never be about things as we once thought when we first picked up this book to read, is it? You have now discovered that pressing towards the mark is totally about you and not about things. It is about being the person you were designed to be, flaws and all, while being completely and confidently secure in your own special identity. It is about being a bright witness to someone who you cross paths with who needs the energy of life in which you hold and flow heavily in.

When you find your strength you are able to stand tall with a grand posture knowing you are being the very best version of you that you can possibly be. It means no longer do you strive with the hearts of men and/or women trying to please them or make them happy while in return all you receive is grief and despair because they refuse to accept the authentic you. It is in this place where you realize you were once a lost cause, a lost soul but now you have been found.

For those of you who are reading my book I must let you know that I must reiterate to you that I am a certified professional life coach who specializes in personal development. As I was coming up and evolving into the woman you see today as "Coach TMB" the things I am sharing with you are the very things I had to learn and implement into my life. This is one of the things that drives me because I see way to many people falling by the wayside of life like I once was just a few years ago. I want to see people become more happier with themselves first before they begin work on other areas of their lives in our coaching partnership. I always preach that you must find balance; spiritually, mentally, and physically. This my friend is the beginning of attaining the strength you need to conquer the mountains and walk through the valley's, which are before you still. Now you are beginning to arm yourself with the weaponry needed to be able to forge forward in your battle to live out the dreams you created that will change the very heart of those who are tied and connected to you.

I need to ensure you are getting fit in all three areas because if you are not, you will not be effective in strategically marketing your product which is you. It is important that you are skilled in communication and delivery of your brand in what you have to offer the world.

I will not think small and say that there is somebody who needs you because I know for a fact that there are many, many people who need you to be effective so you will be able to give them the piece of you they need so they can continue to move forward and live their lives.

My book is not a book on spirituality or religion for there are many of those types of tools out on the market today to help you but what I will say is this. Spiritually you must be balanced... It is imperative you have a place you go to get what your spirit man needs on a continuous basis to survive so you can always be in a healthy place. So I ask the question, what do you do or how do you feed your spirit? And when I ask that question I am not talking about a place of worship where we do religious things but I am asking you where your place of solice is? Where is the place you can pray, meditate, and sit quietly to gain insight and/or direction for yourself and then for what you do? Where? This is so important beloved, and I need for you to wrap your mind around the question I'm asking you because it is very important to your wellbeing of life. Find your place of centering.

Next I have to ask you, are getting your balance mentally? Who are you talking to and who are you receiving wise counsel from? How are you sharpening your tools? These questions are very important because we all need a safe place as we are moving forward moving mountains out of people's way. Who are those individuals you are able to earnestly talk to and be plain ole you and say whatever is on your mind? You need this beloved, this is healthy and it's a part of being whole. You need to be able to download often and get all of the junk out so when it's time to get the good stuff in, there is room for your mind to embrace and take it completely in. The second part of the mental piece was who are you receiving wise counsel from. I implore you to not be a lone ranger any more my friend. I know and I understand fully that you cannot share your vision and dreams with everyone but you need wise counsel who can be a sounding board for your ideas and who will help you think it through thoroughly. They are in position to challenge and stretch you so you become an even sharper version of yourself. This is healthy. This is balance. This is needed in your life. Also to add, this is the importance of sharpening your tools. As I talk about this I want you to understand the importance of knowing in detail what you do. You must be skilled in your craft! If you are going to affect the lives of people in a positive and effective way in the way you were designed to do it, you must know about your area of expertise in detail. Do you understand what I am sharing with you? You must read. You must study. You must know the trends, etc. about what you do because people are looking to you as being the expert in the field. When they think about that certain piece of information or thing that they need, your name pops in their head and they contact you. This is what I am talking about!

The last thing I must challenge you on is your balance in the physical department. These days everybody is so busy, so busy where they do not even value the importance of themselves by learning how to create time to take care of themselves physically through some type of cardiovascular activities and eating better to live... I could bombard you with all types of statistics on where folks are in America when it comes this subject but I won't because if what I have said already has you a little on edge then I know I am on point in my delivery. Let me ask you a question reader? If you only get to live once and we only get one body to take care of then why do we continue abusing ourselves through the mistreatment of our beautiful precious bodies. Is it really that hard to be mindful of what you are putting in your body via food and drink? Is being good to you better than being good for you? I have to ask you these hard questions because the point I am trying to make is that you need to start paying more attention to yourself and not the things of this world which you think hold precedence above the precious commodity of you, beloved. Stop and take a look at yourself in these areas and you will see you are lacking and it is affecting the rest of the outcomes in your life. This is what I am talking about when I say, *when you find your strength.*

It is important for me to challenge you in your way of thinking now because this right here will be the foundation to the previous chapters you have read. Everything I wrote was on purpose and it makes sense if you really open your mind and listen to what I've shared with you. Some things you will agree with and some you won't and I am totally ok either way it goes but at least now I know firsthand that you are more aware than you were before because I have had a personal one on one with you throughout this book as if I was sitting right there in your kitchen at the table having a candid session with you.

What will you do with the thoughts that I have shared with you throughout the pages of this book. Will you take some of these observations seriously? If you need to change, will you? If you need to act on something, will you? Will you learn how to live your life on purpose and not by happenstance? Will your voice ever be heard or will your story ever be told? I must ask these questions towards the end because I need your mind to really process the matter. I am a coach remember, and this is what I do. My coaching style is real life with real talk to real people with real issues who are searching for wholeness which will lead to their personal greatness. When you find your strength this is what begins to take place in your life beloved. You begin to take yourself and your life a lot more seriously. You begin to ask yourself the hard questions and come up with real answers to them. You have conversations with those close to you about the contents shared with in this book.

I need for people to come to a place of being real with themselves when it comes to their own lives. Stop blaming others or circumstances for why you are where you are today if you are not making any kind of tangible positive impact within your life that pours over into the lives of others who you were specifically called to serve. Does that make sense? Sure it does. That is the reason why you are having such a hard time process what I have just shared with you. You are a life changer and a world changer! When will you finally embrace it and walk it out? Many of us are broken in so many different ways and in so many different places in our lives. We have got to come to a place of wholeness, which will be the key to our own personal success. One of the reasons why I felt this chapter probably would be the most important is because it is about reflecting on you the person and not looking at all of the extenuating circumstances in our lives surrounding us. Now I am calling you to action and requesting you begin to look at yourself, you know the man or woman in the mirror theory. There are some things within yourself that have to change first and the change will always start and end with you no matter what you may be doing in your life at this very moment. The reason I feel so strongly about this is because how will you be effective in whatever you may have been positioned to do in your life if you continue to sweep your personal self along with your issues under the rug and not deal. Most people do that and look at how messy their lives are. You will not do that anymore. You will stop to take a real look at yourself and make the necessary adjustments in life now. You will only be able to fake it through so long before it catches up with you. The reason I say this is because you are pressing so hard and so fast towards your so called mark that you feel is going to bring you the fulfillment you have been looking and longing for so long that when you finally get it, you will immediately realize there is still something missing. We as people must understand we will not find happiness or completeness in things or in people for that matter; it must come from a peace within you. Remember I shared that at the beginning of this chapter? Have peace in your life is so important. It is your hot commodity that you cannot afford to loose again.

Open up your heart and mind my friend. Take many reflective moments after you read this book and begin to search yourself completely inside out to see what is really going on with you so you can deal with those unresolved issues whatever they may be, heal, and move forward. Remember your ultimate goal is to be the very best version of you that you can be, right? So with that being said, it means you have to get with yourself and have a conference looking at the good and the bad while moving your way through in the midst of it all. Take what I am sharing to you into consideration because these secrets I am sharing with you will take you to that place called "there" in your life. When you learn, process, and implement some of the methods I've share with you your life will begin to become what you dreamed and thought it would be as you press towards your mark for real now.

It is important to understand the driving forces behind all of the things you do that I've talked about in this book is entitled Pressing Towards The Mark- It's Not What You Think because as you really begin to search yourself you will soon find out that what you thought would bring you joy and happiness really doesn't. What you thought would bring you fulfillment really doesn't. All that you have obtained and achieved really didn't make you feel any better. The money, the cars, the men or the women, the career, the sex, none of that brought you what you thought it was going to bring you. It wasn't what you thought it would be. However, you have now discovered that when you find your strength, which facilitates your press towards the mark, you begin accurately hitting your targets in life while you are changing and impacting the lives of many, many people around you. The key for you was to find a balance mentally, spiritually, and physically. You did the hard work of discovering and uncovering the real authentic you by getting a cure that healed you of your own identity crisis. You are in order, your life is in order, your relationship with your spouse and children are in order, while living in your singleness you get yourself in order, and even when you don't have the support of your family you have a circle of influence supporting you and helping you to maintain that order. Why does all this have to happen and is of the utmost importance? Well, you beloved have now discovered that as you press towards the mark-it is not what you thought it would be.

Moment of Reflection

"It's not who you think you are that holds you back but it is who you think you're not"

Author Unknown

It is my sincere hope that this book has helped you in many ways re-frame how you see yourself and your life. I hope you begin to learn how to treasure the beautiful and authentic real gift of you. Reading my book will not go in vain and I pray that as you begin to meditate on some of the thoughts I shared your life would surely change for the better. I want to thank you from the bottom of my heart for reading this book to its entirety. Just knowing you took time to earnestly read something I have penned truly means the world to me in more ways than you will ever know.

About the Author

Coach Toresa M. Blakely has always had a passion to inspire, challenge, and empower people into learning how to live their lives on purpose and not by happenstance. She has a successful thriving life coaching consultancy and hosts an internet radio talk show which airs on a weekly basis. She is a highly sought after speaker and mentor to many.

For more information on Toresa M. Blakely, aka "Coach TMB" or to schedule her as a speaker, workshop leader, or consultant, please visit
www.coachtmb.com

www.ingramcontent.com/pod-product-compliance
Lightning Source LLC
LaVergne TN
LVHW021546080426
835509LV00019B/2872